Healthy Eating

Claire Llewellyn

QED Publishing

Copyright © QED Publishing 2006

First published in the UK in 2006 by
QED Publishing
A Quarto Group company
226 City Road
London EC1V 2TT
www.qed-publishing.co.uk

A catalogue record for this book is available from the British Library.

ISBN 1 84538 367 2

Written by Claire Llewellyn
Designed by Susi Martin
Editor Louisa Somerville
Consultant Ruth Miller B.Sc., M.I.Biol., C.Biol.
Illustrations John Haslam
Photographs Michael Wicks

Publisher Steve Evans
Editorial Director Jean Coppendale
Art Director Zeta Davies

Printed and bound in China

Picture credits

Getty images Elyse Lewin p20

Words in **bold** are explained
in the glossary on page 22.

Contents

Food, glorious food!

We all need food to stay alive and keep **healthy**. If we didn't eat, our bodies would stop growing and we wouldn't have the energy to move around.

Star tip

Our bodies need lots of different foods. Eating too much of one thing, such as sweets or chips, can be bad for you.

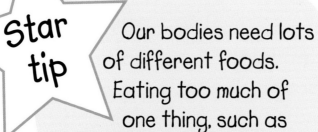

Without food and water your body would s-l-o-w d-o-w-n and stop!

Do it! The food and drink we eat is called our **diet**. Write down everything that you have eaten and drunk in the last two days. Did you eat lots of different foods – or mostly the same?

A little of everything

Imagine being a sheep and eating grass all day long! Our diet contains different foods to give us what we need to grow, keep **active** and stay healthy. This is called a **balanced diet**.

Star tip

Eat different kinds of foods at every meal. Then you'll be eating a balanced diet.

Fish, meat, cheese and eggs help our bodies to grow.

Fruit and vegetables help to keep us healthy.

Bread, pasta and potatoes give us the energy to be active.

Salad sandwich

Make it!

Ask an adult to help you to make a balanced meal. Pile some tuna or grated cheese onto brown bread or pitta and add some crunchy salad. Finish with fruit or yoghurt and a drink of fruit juice or milk. Delicious and healthy!

Fruit and vegetables

We need to eat lots of fruit and vegetables. They contain **vitamins**, which help us grow and keep us healthy.

Which fruit and vegetables do you like best?

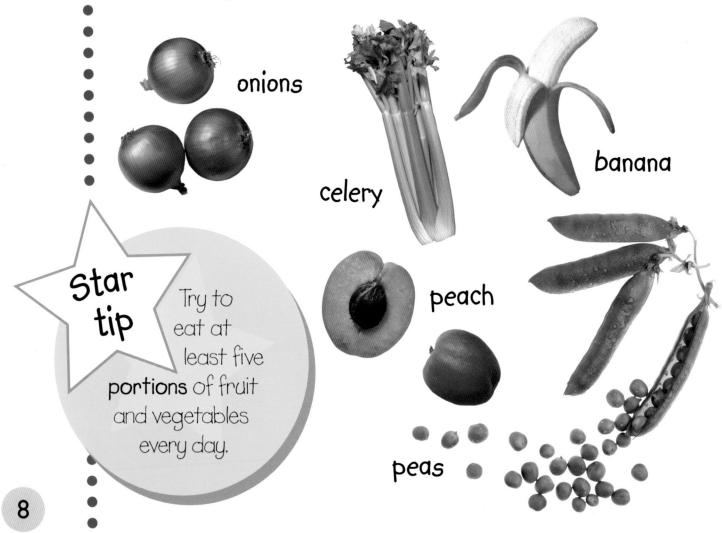

onions

celery

banana

peach

peas

Star tip Try to eat at least five **portions** of fruit and vegetables every day.

Do it!

Bite into a crisp apple and a stick of celery. How do they smell and taste? Which other fruit and vegetables can you eat raw?

Make it!

Fruit kebab

Why not make a fruit kebab! Ask an adult to cut up different-coloured fruits and then you can thread one piece at a time onto a cocktail stick.

Which fruits need peeling or slicing? How do they look, taste and smell?

Energy foods

Every day we need to eat food to give us energy. Foods such as bread, rice, pasta and potatoes give us the most energy.

We need these foods so we can run, jump, skip or swim. Being active is good for our bodies.

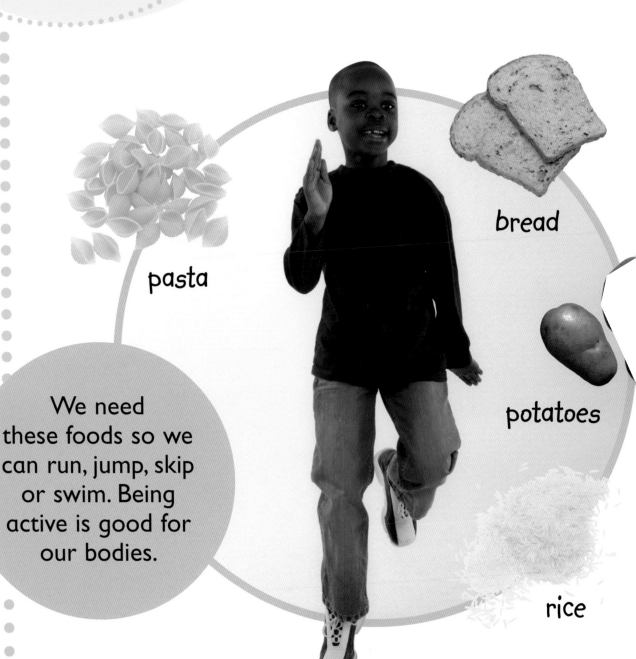

pasta

bread

potatoes

rice

Make it!

Baked potato

1. Clean a big potato and ask an adult to bake it in the oven until it is soft.

2. When it is cooked, ask the adult to cut it in half for you as it will be very hot.

3. Fill it with one of these foods.

What other fillings could you use?

Next time try a sweet potato. They're delicious!

cheese

sour cream

tuna

You're sweet enough

We can also get energy from sugary foods. Fizzy drinks, biscuits, sweets and ice cream all contain sugar. But if you eat too much sugar your diet won't be balanced.

Eating lots of sugary foods is very bad for your teeth. They could **decay**.

Do it!

Compare a fizzy orange drink with fresh orange juice. The fizzy drink is so sugary that it will make the fresh juice taste quite sharp.

Sugar swap

One or two days a week, swap a sweet snack for something healthier.

Which of these would you choose?

yoghurt

dried banana

apple

dried fruits and nuts

Make it!

Fruit smoothie

A fruit smoothie is a treat you can enjoy that does not have a lot of added sugar. Choose a banana, some strawberries or peaches. Ask an adult to whizz them in a **blender** with some low-fat yoghurt or milk. Add an ice cube for extra-cold froth.

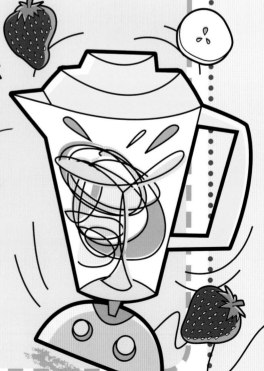

Healthy snacks

Do you eat crisps, peanuts, sausages and other salty, fatty foods often?

Do it!

Next time you have sausages, ask an adult to grill them instead of frying them. That way, you eat less fat!

If you eat too many of these foods too often, you'll have an unhealthy diet.

It's better to eat them as treats now and then.

plain popcorn

unsalted peanuts

breadsticks

Star tip

Next time you want a bag of crisps, try one of these snacks instead.

Make it!

Stick 'n' dip

Make a low-salt snack. Ask an adult to peel an avocado and take out the stone. Whizz the avocado in a blender with natural yoghurt and lemon juice.

Now ask an adult to chop carrots, celery and red peppers into bite-size sticks. Scoop up your avocado dip with the healthy dippers.

Drink up!

We should drink at least a litre or two of **fluid** each day to keep our bodies working well.

Try to drink at least a glass of water, milk or fruit juice at every meal.

Don't forget to drink plenty!

Sip it, slurp it, gulp it! Drink six to eight glasses of fluid a day. Your body needs more when the weather is hot or when you have been very active.

Star tip

When we exercise, we **sweat** and our bodies lose water. Always drink some water before and after you exercise.

Make it!

Fruity fizz

Make a fruity, fizzy drink.

Put some ice cubes in a glass, then pour in a little of your favourite juice.

Top up the glass with fizzy water.

Try other fruit juices, too!

How much food?

We should only eat the amount of food our bodies need.

Most of us need three balanced meals, one or two healthy snacks and lots of water each day.

If you're small or **inactive**, you won't need as much food as someone who is BIG or very active.

Star tip

Even while you are asleep, your body uses up energy. To give you the energy to get going in the morning, always eat a good breakfast.

fruit and vegetables

bread, cereals and potatoes

To stay healthy, your body needs more fruit, vegetables, cereals and bread than fat, sugar and meat.

milk and dairy

meat, fish and eggs

fats and sugars

Do it!

Make a big poster showing all the food that you eat in one day. Count up all the fruit and vegetables on your poster. Are there five or more? Did you eat something from each of the sections in the chart above?

What's cooking?

Have a go at cooking! You can see how the food you eat is cooked if you help in the kitchen at home.

An adult must help you to use the cooker and handle hot things, but there are lots of things you can make by yourself.

Do it!

Ask an adult to help you choose a **recipe** from a cookery book or magazine. Then go shopping together for the things you need. Follow the recipe and make the dish.

Now try it out on your family or friends.

roasted squash
- delicious and sweet

peanuts
out of the
shell – fresh
and nutty

Star tip

Try eating
something
new and healthy.
Have you tried
any of these
foods?

mango
- Wow! What a
tangy taste!

It's fun to eat things
you have made
yourself, and your
family will like it, too!

fresh coconut
- sweet and
chewy

21

Glossary

diet the food and drink we usually eat

fluid a liquid, such as water or fruit juice

healthy fit and well

inactive sitting or lying still and not moving around

portion a helping of food

recipe how to make a dish of food

sweat the sticky liquid that comes out of your skin when your body is hot. Sweating helps you to cool down

vitamins substances found in food that help us to stay healthy

active to be moving, working and doing things

balanced diet a diet made up of different kinds of food

blender a machine for mixing food and making it runny

cereals grains such as rice and oats. Breakfast cereal is also made from them

decay to go bad and rot

Index

23

Notes
for parents and teachers

- Look through the book and talk about the pictures. Which of the foods do your children like/not like? Are there any foods that your children have not seen or tried before? If so, would they like to try them?

- Foods come in many different colours. Your children could draw a rainbow of different foods. How many red, orange, yellow, green and blue-violet foods can you think of? Look through cookery books for inspiration.

- Over a meal, discuss the foods you are eating. Can your children remember how each one helps the body? Is your meal balanced? If not, what would make it so?

- There are many different words to describe the way food looks, tastes and feels (golden, sweet, slippery and so on). Make a list of food words with your children. Encourage your children to draw a picture to accompany each word.

- Ask your children to think up a new sandwich for a packed lunch. Go to the shops and let your children choose some unusual bread. Together, can you think of a new filling?

- Which are your children's favourite/least favourite foods? You could do a survey of the likes and dislikes of several children. Which foods are the most/least popular?

- Look at the lunch menu at school for a week. Ask your children to say which meals are the healthier choices. Why are the other meals less healthy?

- Have a 'Try A New Taste' day. Buy some new foods that your children have never tasted. Display them all and try some. What does each one smell and taste like?

- Do a project on your children's favourite meal. Together, find out which foods it is made from. How and where is the food grown? Help your children to make notes about this.

- What do people in other countries eat for breakfast? Using books and the Internet, find out about breakfasts around the world. How are they different from your usual breakfast? How are they the same?

- Visit the supermarket and look at the labels on different fruit and vegetables together to see where the produce grows.

- Do your children know the alphabet? If they do, play an ABC memory game with different foods, for example: 'I went to the shop and I bought an apple.' 'I went to the shop and I bought an apple and some bread' etc.

- Using books and the Internet, find out more about how sugar harms our teeth. Help your children to make a factsheet about this.

Before undertaking any activity which involve eating, always check whether the children in your care have any food allergies. In a classroom situation, prior written permission from all the parents may be required.